BRAIN GAMES
for Clever Kids®

8 Year Olds ➚

Puzzles and solutions
by Dr Gareth Moore
B.Sc (Hons) M.Phil Ph.D

Illustrations and cover
artwork by Chris Dickason

Designed by Imago Create

BRAIN GAMES
for Clever Kids®
8 Year Olds

BUSTER BOOKS

First published in Great Britain in 2024 by Buster Books,
an imprint of Michael O'Mara Books Limited,
9 Lion Yard, Tremadoc Road, London SW4 7NQ

W www.mombooks.com/buster

f Buster Books

X @BusterBooks

⌾ @buster_books

Clever Kids is a trade mark of Michael O'Mara Books Limited.

Puzzles and solutions © Gareth Moore

Illustrations and layouts © Buster Books 2024

A CIP catalogue record for this book is available from the British Library.

ISBN: 978-1-78055-938-4

2 4 6 8 10 9 7 5 3

This product is made of material from well-managed, FSC®-certified
forests and other controlled sources. The manufacturing processes
conform to the environmental regulations of the country of origin.

This book was printed in November 2024 by
CPI Group (UK) Ltd, Croydon, CR0 4YY.

MIX
Paper | Supporting
responsible forestry
FSC® C171272

INTRODUCTION

Get ready to push your brain to the limit with these fun-filled games!

Take your pick of 101 puzzles. You can complete them in any order you like and work through at your own pace.

Start each puzzle by reading the instructions. Sometimes this is the hardest part of the puzzle, so don't worry if you have to read the instructions a few times to be clear on what they mean.

Once you know what to do, it's time to battle your way to the answer. Time yourself completing each puzzle, and write your time in the box at the top of each page. For an extra challenge, you can come back to the puzzles at a later date and see if you can complete them even faster.

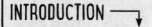
There's a notes and scribbles section at the back that you can use to help you work out the answers.

If you really struggle with a puzzle, take a look at the solutions at the back to see how it works, then try it again later and see if you can work it out the second time round.

Good luck, and have fun!

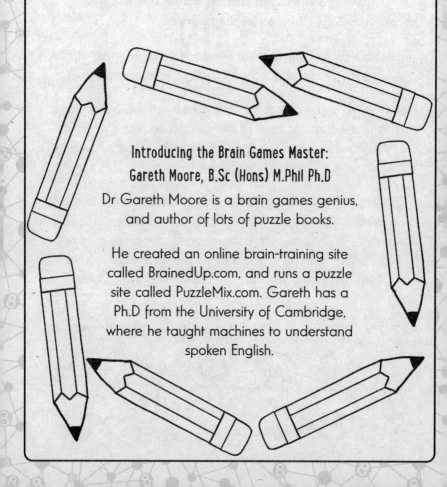

Introducing the Brain Games Master:
Gareth Moore, B.Sc (Hons) M.Phil Ph.D

Dr Gareth Moore is a brain games genius, and author of lots of puzzle books.

He created an online brain-training site called BrainedUp.com, and runs a puzzle site called PuzzleMix.com. Gareth has a Ph.D from the University of Cambridge, where he taught machines to understand spoken English.

Three plates have been dropped and each has split into two. Can you draw lines to rejoin the halves into their original complete plates?

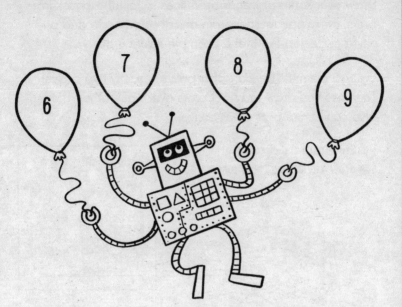

Your friend has challenged you to pick up a selection of balloons whose numbers add up to various totals. Which balloons do you choose for each total? The first one is done for you as an example. Each balloon can be used no more than once per total.

16 = (7) + (9)   17 = ◯ + ◯

13 = ◯ + ◯   21 = ◯ + ◯ + ◯

Draw over some of the dashed lines to join the circles into pairs. Every pair must contain one shaded circle and one white circle, just like in the example solution below.

Every circle must be part of a pair of exactly two circles. The lines you draw must not cross over each other. They also can't cross over other circles.

Tip: Start with the circles that only have one other circle they could connect to.

a)

b)

c)

Start at the 'X' and then follow the arrows in the order
given, moving one square in the direction shown for each
arrow in turn. At which letter do you end up?

→ ↑ ← ← ↓ ↓ → ↓ ← ←

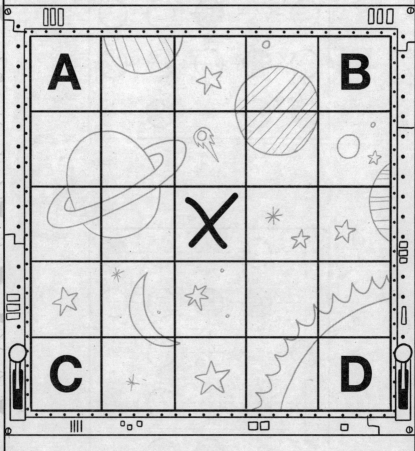

The answer is: ....

Join all of the dots with straight lines, starting at 4 (marked with a star) and then adding 4 at each step until you reach the final dot, which is hollow. What is revealed?

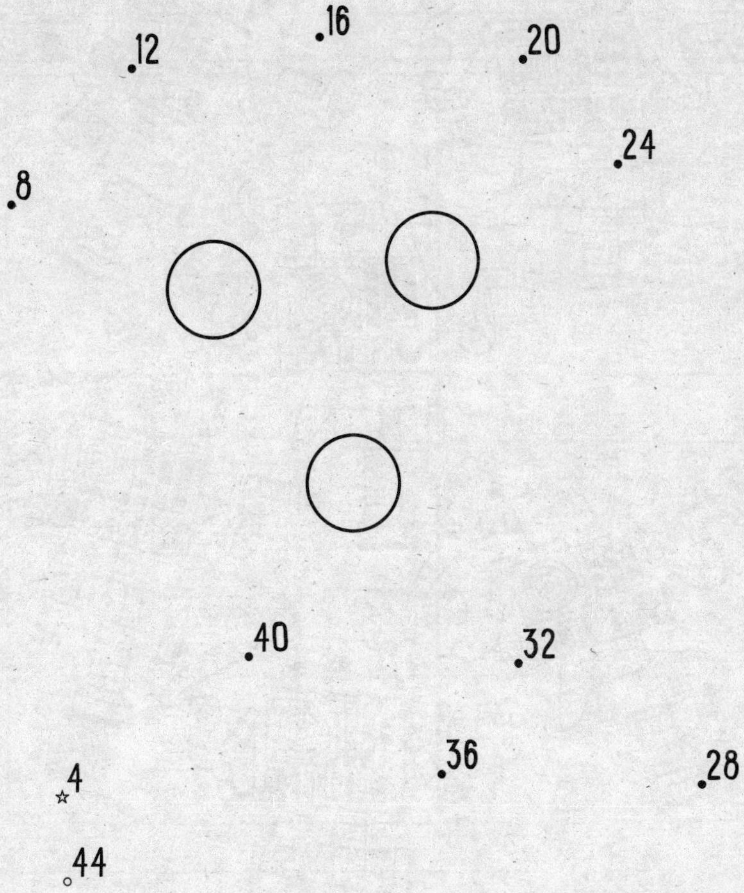

.12

.16

.20

.24

.8

.40

.32

4
☆

.36

.28

○44

These six pictures look similar, but there are in fact exactly two of each design. Can you find the identical pairs, then draw lines to join them?

One of the following numbers doesn't fit in with the rest. Can you work out which is the odd-one-out, and say why?

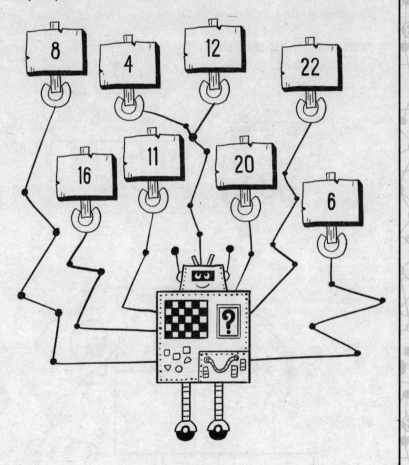

The odd-one-out is ...., because ....

....

In the number pyramid below, each number is equal to the result of adding together the two numbers directly beneath it. Can you fill in the empty boxes in the other number pyramids so that they also follow the same rule?

Here's an example to show what a complete pyramid looks like:

	15	
7		8
4	3	5

a)

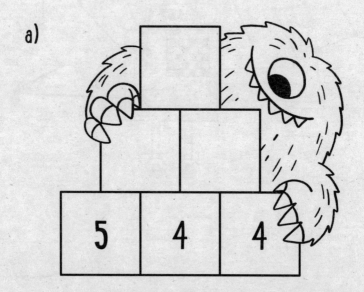

5	4	4	

b)

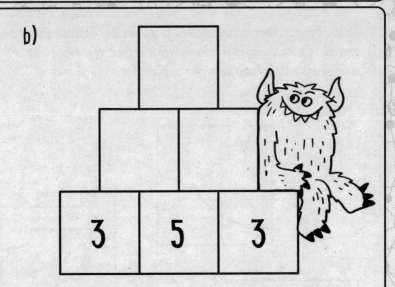

| 3 | 5 | 3 |

In this last puzzle you will need to subtract numbers to work out the missing values.

c)

	9	
		4
		2

These four tiles can be arranged into a 2×2 square to reveal a picture of a number. What is that number? You don't need to rotate any of the tiles.

The number is: ....

Three of the pieces remain to be placed in this jigsaw puzzle.
Can you draw lines to show where each piece should go?

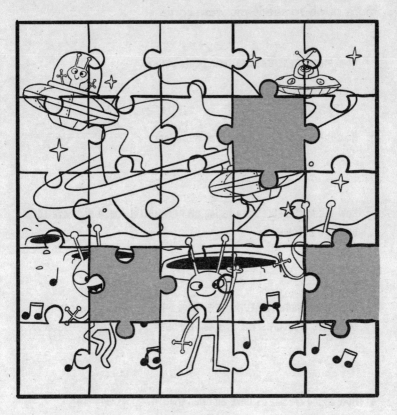

Take a look at the monsters opposite, and answer the following questions as quickly as you can – then check more slowly to see if you were correct.

a) How many creatures are facing this page?

....

b) How many creatures have 8 or more legs?

....

c) How many creatures are facing away from this page **and** have three or more antennae?

....

d) How many more creatures are there with straight antennae than there are creatures with curved horns?

....

e) How many creatures have an open mouth, spots and are looking up?

....

f) Which creature has the greatest total number of legs plus antennae?

....

🕑 TIME ....

Which of the following shapes is the odd-one-out, and why?

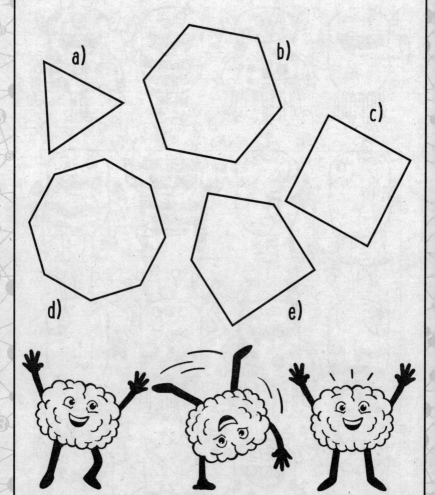

a)

b)

c)

d)

e)

The odd-one-out is ...., because ....

....

Can you find each of these eight numbers in the grid? They can be written in any direction, including diagonally, and may read forwards or backwards. One is found for you already, as an example.

212765   383644   67005   873051

340856   431208   741919   887696

4	0	1	5	0	3	7	8
7	3	3	1	8	2	7	8
5	8	1	3	9	6	9	7
2	6	6	2	5	3	4	6
1	4	2	8	0	1	6	9
4	6	0	5	9	8	9	6
8	4	2	1	2	7	6	5
3	4	9	5	0	0	7	6

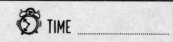
How many rectangles, of various sizes, can you count in the following picture?

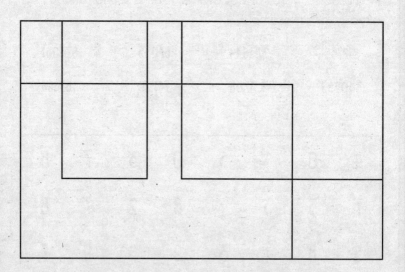

Don't forget the large one all around the outside!

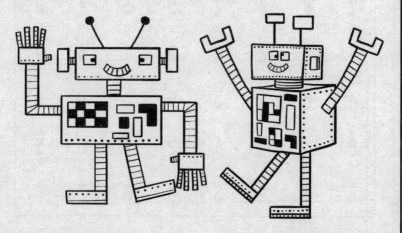

The answer is: ....

Sam, Emma and Patrick each have a pet dog, and each pet dog has a different collar. You also know that:

· The three dogs are called Dexter, Pickle and Rover

· The three collars are one of green, blue or red

· Rover is Sam's dog

· Dexter has a blue collar

· Patrick's dog has a red collar

Now can you work out:

a) Who is Dexter's owner? ....

b) Which collar does Pickle have? ....

c) What is Patrick's dog called? ....

You can use the table below to help you keep track of your working:

Owner Name	Dog Name	Collar Colour

Can you circle the eight differences between these two images?

Which of the three options, 1 to 3, is a perfect mirror reflection of the image on the left of each row?

a)

1)   2)   3)

The answer is: ....

b)

 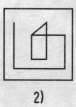 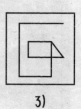

1)   2)   3)

The answer is: ....

c)

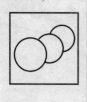 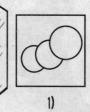 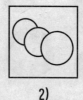

1)   2)   3)

The answer is: ....

How quickly can you find your way through this maze? Start at the arrow at the top.

These four pictures might all look the same, but one is slightly different to the others. Can you find and then circle the odd-one-out?

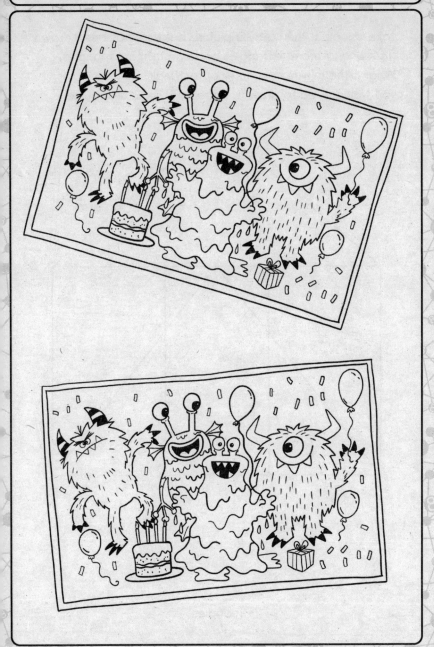

⏱ TIME ....

Take a look at the tent-like picture below. It has been drawn from one or more rectangles and one or more triangles. What is the minimum number of rectangles and triangles you would need to draw to recreate this picture yourself?

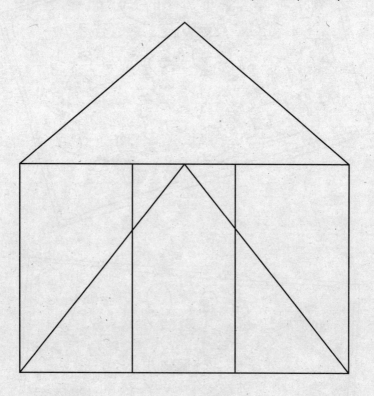

.... Rectangles

.... Triangles

Imagine rotating each of these shapes as shown by the arrow beneath it: 90° clockwise, 180°, and 90° anticlockwise as shown. Which of the options, 1 to 3, will result for each?

a)

b)

c)

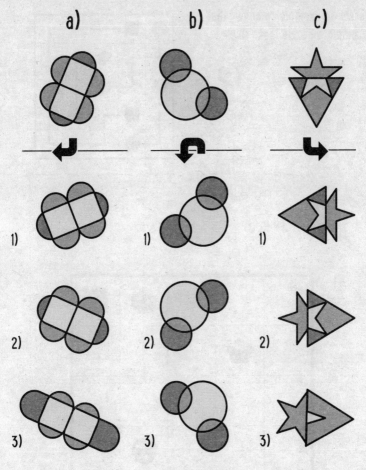

1)

2)

3)

The answer is:

The answer is:

The answer is:

....

....

....

Draw lines to join each pair of identical shapes, just like in the example solution below. Only one line can enter each square, and lines can't be drawn diagonally.

Here's an example to show what a complete puzzle looks like:

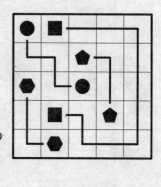

a)

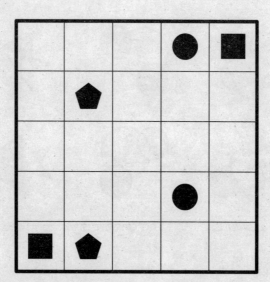

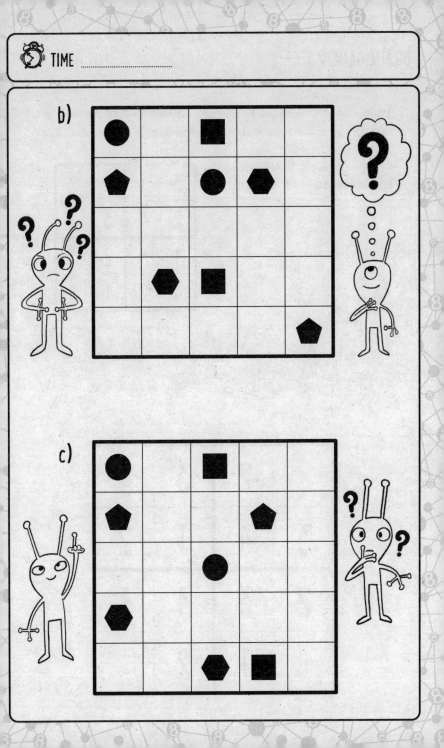

Write 1, 2, 3 or 4 into each empty square so that no number repeats in any row, column or bold-lined 2×2 box.

Here's an example solved puzzle, so you can see how it works:

3	1	4	2
2	4	3	1
1	3	2	4
4	2	1	3

a)

	2	3	
3	4	1	2
2	3	4	1
	1	2	

b)

2	3	1	
4			2
1			3
	2	4	1

c)

1			2
	2	4	
	1	2	
2			4

Can you draw either an 'X' or an 'O' into every empty box of each puzzle so that no lines of 4 'X's or 'O's in a row are formed in any direction, including diagonally?

In the example puzzle below, if you were to draw an 'O' in any of the empty boxes then you'd form a line of 4 'O's. This means the solution must be as shown, with an 'X' in each of those boxes.

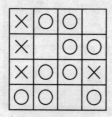

Example puzzle

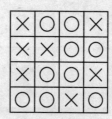

Example solution

a)

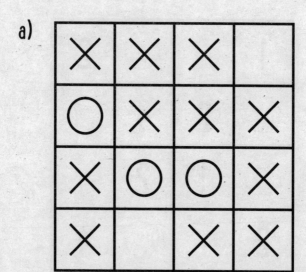

b)

c)

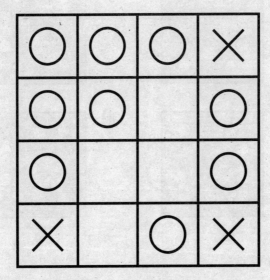

⏰ TIME ....

Imagine folding this piece of paper in half as shown, then punching four holes in it, as shown. If you unfold it again, which of the four options, a to d, below will result?

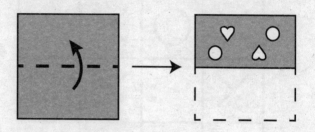

a)
b)
c)
d)

The answer is: ....

Take a look at the robot at the top of the page, then at each of the four possible silhouettes beneath. Can you circle the one silhouette which exactly matches the outline of the robot?

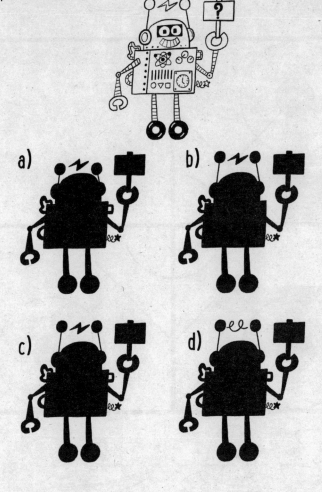

a)

b)

c)

d)

The answer is: ....

Can you draw in the empty box below to complete the pattern correctly?

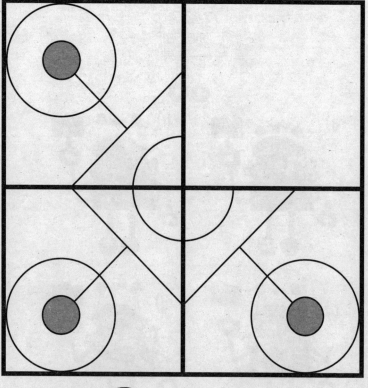

Take a good look at the four monsters on this page.
Once you think you will remember what they look like, turn
the page and then circle the two new monsters that have
been added.

Can you draw the six loose dominoes onto the shaded tiles to complete this domino chain? Whenever two domino ends are next to one another, they must have the same number of dots.

Can you work out which number should come next in each of the following mathematical sequences?

a)   1   3   5   7   9   ....

b)   22   20   18   16   14   ....

c)   90   80   70   60   50   ....

d)   4   9   14   19   24   ....

e)   1   2   4   8   16   ....

Shade in each square according to the key below to reveal a hidden picture.

1 = green   2 = blue   3 = yellow   4 = red   5 = black

1	1	1	1	1	2	2	2	2	2	1	1	1	1	1
1	1	1	2	2	2	3	3	3	2	2	2	1	1	1
1	1	2	2	3	3	3	3	3	3	3	2	2	1	1
1	2	2	3	3	3	3	3	3	3	3	3	2	2	1
1	2	2	3	4	4	3	3	3	4	4	3	2	2	5
2	2	3	3	4	4	3	3	3	4	4	3	3	2	5
2	2	3	3	3	3	3	3	3	3	3	3	3	2	5
2	2	3	3	3	3	3	3	3	3	3	3	3	2	5
2	2	3	3	3	3	3	3	3	3	3	3	3	2	5
1	2	2	3	4	4	3	3	3	4	4	3	2	2	5
1	2	2	3	3	4	4	4	4	4	3	3	2	2	5
1	1	2	2	3	3	3	3	3	3	3	2	2	5	5
1	1	1	2	2	3	3	3	3	2	2	2	5	5	1
1	1	1	1	2	2	2	2	2	2	2	5	5	1	1
1	1	1	1	1	2	2	2	2	2	5	5	1	1	1

Three plates have been dropped and each has split into two. Can you draw lines to rejoin the halves into their original complete plates?

The shape shown to the right has been hidden in one of the four images below, but which one? The answer must contain all of the black lines which make up the original image, but they may have been rotated – or had extra lines added.

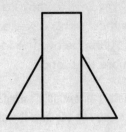

a)

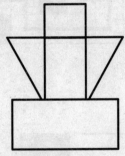

b)

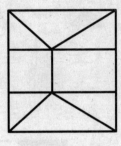

c)

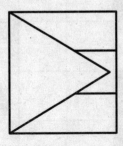

d)

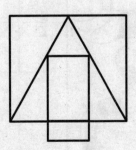

The answer is: _____

Draw lines to make a loop which visits every white square without using any diagonal lines, just like in the example solution below. The loop can't cross itself or use any square more than once.

Here's an example solved puzzle, so you can see how it works:

a)

🕐 TIME _____

Shade in this image according to the key below to reveal a hidden picture.

1 = yellow   2 = light blue   3 = red   4 = orange

5 = pink   6 = purple   7 = light green   8 = dark green

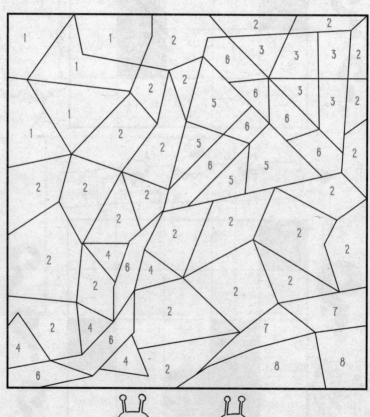

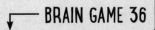
Take a look at this picture, until you think you will remember it. Then, once you are ready, turn the page and redraw it as well as you can.

Once complete, turn back and see how you did.

Starting on a circle which contains a 1, can you trace a route along the lines to 2, 3, 4 and then 5 in that order, without visiting any number more than once?

Jack is going to market to sell his cow. He hopes that someone at the market will give him some gold coins for the cow.

The first person he speaks to at the market says he will give Jack some gold coins:

> 'The number of gold coins I will offer you is between 1 and 10. The number is an even number, and it's also in the 3-times table.'

a) How many gold coins does the first person offer Jack?

....

Jack then speaks to a second person at the market, who offers him magic beans instead:

> 'I can give you a number of magic beans between 1 and 10 – and I can give you more magic beans than the number of gold coins you have just been offered. The number of magic beans is also in the 3-times table, but is not an even number.'

b) How many magic beans does the second person offer Jack?

....

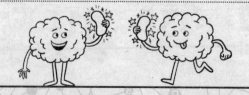

Which of the three options, 1 to 3, is a perfect mirror reflection of the image at the top of each row?

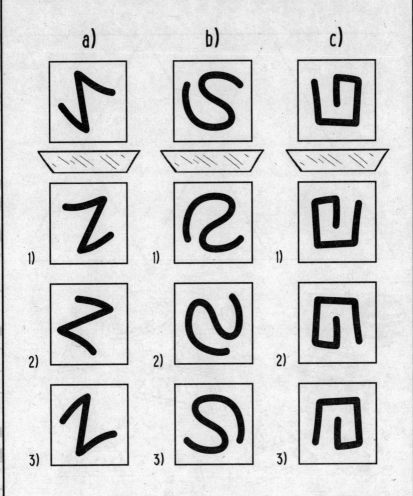

a)

b)

c)

1)

2)

3)

The answer is:

....

The answer is:

....

The answer is:

....

How many triangles, of various sizes, can you count in the following picture?

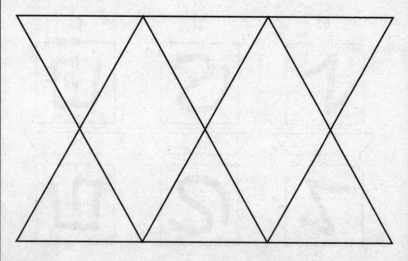

The answer is: ....

Can you find each of these eight numbers in the grid?
They can be written in any direction, including
diagonally, and may read forwards or backwards.

236150	324799	444171	594476
248009	326381	464665	690452

0	7	9	7	0	2	1	5
3	5	6	6	4	8	6	6
0	4	1	8	3	6	7	9
1	1	0	6	4	2	4	9
9	0	2	6	3	9	4	7
9	3	4	2	4	2	9	4
6	9	0	4	5	2	5	2
6	4	4	4	1	7	1	3

One of the following numbers doesn't fit in with the rest.
Can you work out which is the odd-one-out, and say why?

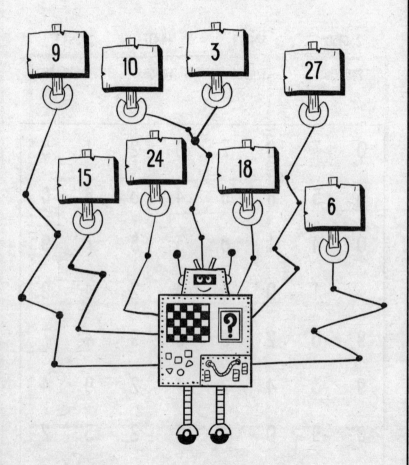

9   10   3   27

15   24   18   6

The odd-one-out is ...., because ....

....

Can you draw in the empty box below to complete the pattern correctly?

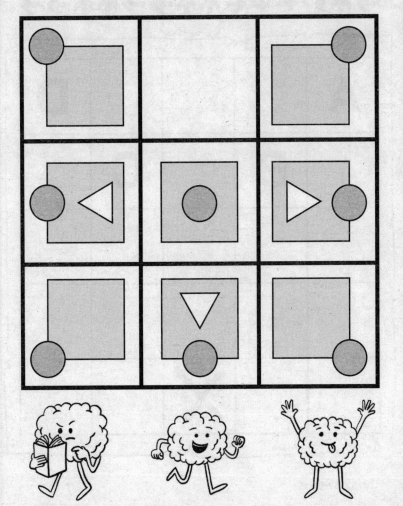

Start at the 'X' and then follow the arrows in the order given, moving one square in the direction shown for each arrow in turn. At which letter do you end up?

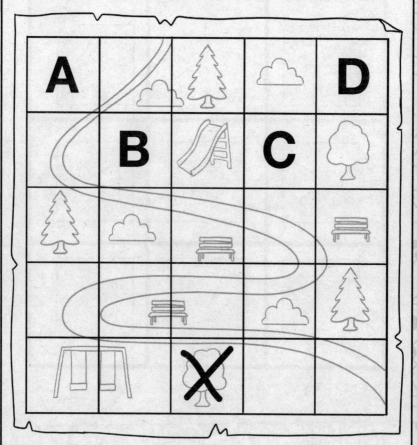

The answer is: _____

Your friend has challenged you to pick up a selection of balloons whose numbers add up to various totals. Which balloons do you choose for each total? Each balloon can only be used once per total. The first one is done for you as an example.

Totals:

17 = (7) + (10)   13 = 🎈 + 🎈

11 = 🎈 + 🎈   18 = 🎈 + 🎈 + 🎈

Can you draw either an 'X' or an 'O' into every empty box of each puzzle so that no lines of 4 'X's or 'O's in a row are formed in any direction, including diagonally?

Here's an example solved puzzle, so you can see how it works:

a)

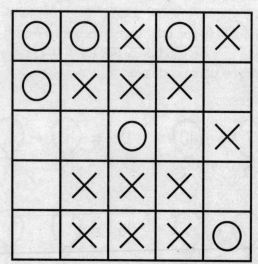

b)

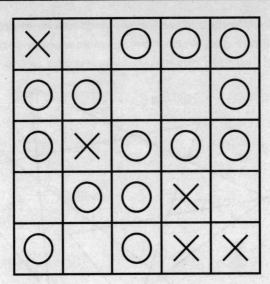

c)

O	X	O	O	
O		O	O	
X	O		O	X
X	O	O	X	X
O	O	X		

⏰ TIME ....

Take a look at the picture below, which has been drawn using just triangles. What is the minimum number of triangles you would need to draw to recreate this picture yourself?

.... triangles

Take a good look at the five items of clothing on this page. Once you think you will remember what they are, turn the page and read the instruction.

Two of the items have been removed. Can you draw them in the empty boxes below?

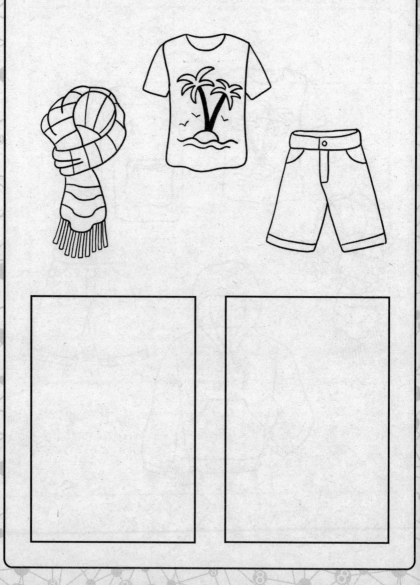

These four pieces need to be placed in this jigsaw puzzle. Can you draw lines to show where each piece should go?

These four pictures might all look the same, but one is slightly different to the others. Can you find and then circle the odd-one-out?

Write 1, 2, 3 or 4 into each empty square so that no number repeats in any row, column or bold-lined 2×2 box.

Here's an example solved puzzle, so you can see how it works:

3	1	4	2
2	4	3	1
1	3	2	4
4	2	1	3

a)

2			1
	1	4	
	3	2	
4			3

b)

	4	2	
2			1
4			2
	2	1	

c)

		4	
1			
			3
	2		

⏱ TIME ....

Which of the following shapes is the odd-one-out, and why?

a)

b)

c)

d)

e)

f)

The odd-one-out is .... , because ....

....

The shape at the top of the page has been hidden in one of the four images below, but which one? The answer must contain all of the black lines which make up the original image, but they may have been rotated – or had extra lines added.

a)

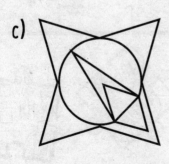

b)

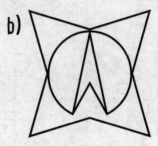

c)

d)

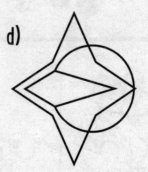

The answer is: ....

These four pieces need to be placed in this jigsaw puzzle. Can you draw lines to show where each piece should go?

Take a good look at the six objects on this page. Once you think you will remember what they are, turn the page and then circle the two new objects that have been added.

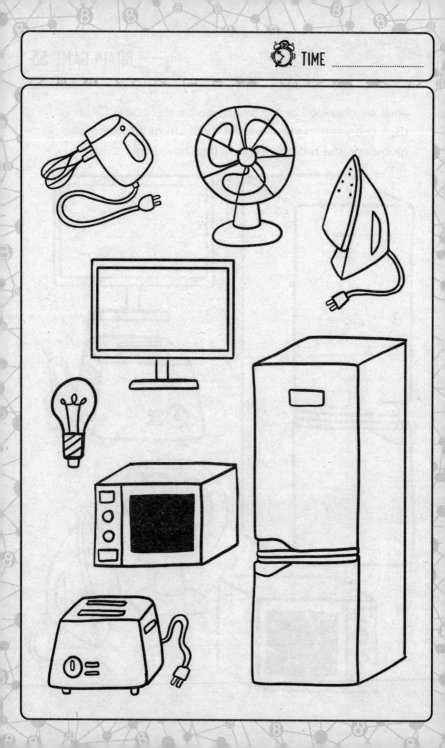

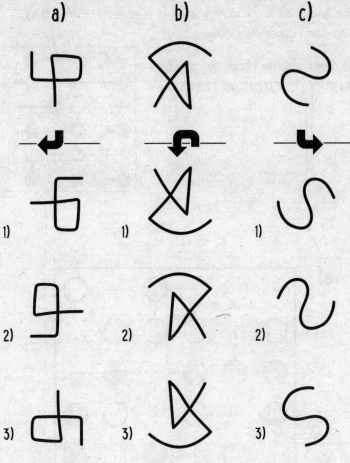

Imagine rotating each of these shapes as shown by the arrow beneath it: 90° clockwise, 180°, and 90° anticlockwise as shown. Which of the options, 1 to 3, will result?

a)

b)

c)

1)

1)

1)

2)

2)

2)

3)

3)

3)

The answer is:

The answer is:

The answer is:

....

....

....

Draw over some of the dashed lines to join the circles into pairs. Every pair must contain one shaded circle and one white circle, just like in the example solution below.
Every circle must be part of a pair of exactly two circles. The lines you draw must not cross over each other. They also can't cross over other circles.

Tip: Start with the circles that only have one other circle they could connect to.

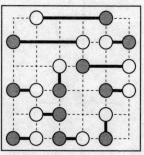

a)

b)

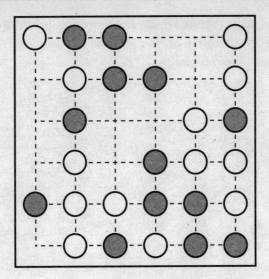

c)

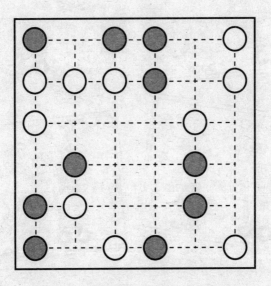

These six pictures look similar, but there are in fact exactly two of each design. Can you find the identical pairs, then draw lines to join them?

How quickly can you find your way all the way through this maze? Start at the arrow at the top.

Start

Finish

One of the following numbers doesn't fit in with the rest. Can you work out which is the odd-one-out, and say why?

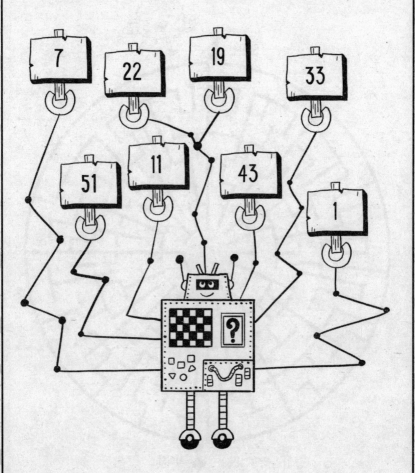

The odd-one-out is ...., because ....

....

Join all of the dots with straight lines, starting at 3 (marked with a star) and then adding 3 at each step until you reach the final dot, which is hollow. What is revealed?

○75   ☆3

．66   ．72 ．6 ．12   ．15

．63

69． ．9

．60

．57   ．21

．54   ．24

．42 ．36

．51   ．27

．39

．48   ．45   ．33   ．30

In the number pyramid below, each number is equal to the result of adding together the two numbers directly beneath it. Can you fill in the empty boxes in the other number pyramids so that they also follow the same rule? You will need to both add and subtract to work them all out.

Here's an example to show what a complete pyramid looks like:

| 27 |
14	13
7	7	6
4	3	4	2

a)

7		
	2	5	3

b)

A pyramid of blocks. Top row: one empty block. Second row: empty block, block with **13**. Third row: **8**, **6**, empty block. Bottom row: empty, empty, empty, **4**.

c)

A pyramid of blocks. Top row: one empty block. Second row: empty block, block with **18**. Third row: **10**, empty block, **8**. Bottom row: empty, empty, **5**, empty.

These six pictures might all look the same, but one is slightly different to the others. Can you find and then circle the odd-one-out?

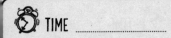

Shade in this image according to the key below to reveal a hidden picture.

1 = light blue   2 = dark blue   3 = yellow   4 = orange

5 = red   6 = pink   7 = purple   8 = light brown

9 = dark brown   10 = grey   11 = black   12 = green

Take a good look at the six pieces of cutlery on this page. Once you think you will remember what they are, turn the page and read the instruction.

Two of the items have been removed. Can you draw them in the empty boxes below?

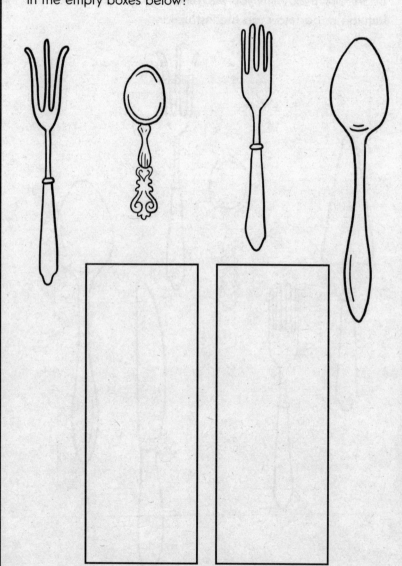

Imagine folding a square of paper in half twice, then cutting out the three shapes as shown. If you now fully unfold the paper, which of the following will result?

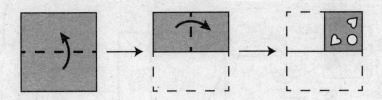

a)
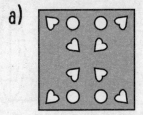

b)
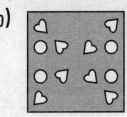

c)
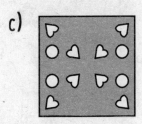

d)
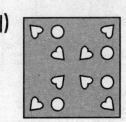

The answer is: ....

These four tiles can be arranged into a 2x2 square to reveal a picture of a letter. What is that letter? You don't need to rotate any of the tiles.

The answer is: ....

Take a look at this picture until you think you will remember it. Then, once you are ready, turn the page and redraw it as well as you can.

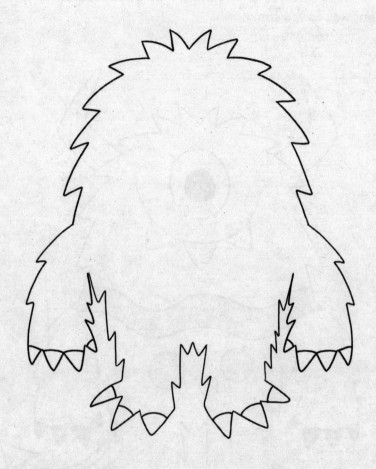

Once complete, check back and see how you did.

Starting on a circle which contains a 1, can you trace a route along the lines to 2, 3, 4 and then 5 in that order, without visiting any number more than once?

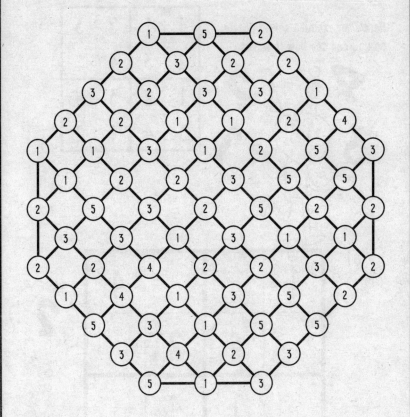

Write 1, 2, 3 or 4 into each empty square so that no number repeats in any row, column or bold-lined 2x2 box. All even numbers (2 and 4) must be written in the grey squares, while all odd numbers (1 and 3) must be written in the white squares.

Here's an example solved puzzle, so you can see how it works:

4	1	2	3
2	3	4	1
1	2	3	4
3	4	1	2

a)

1			4
	4	2	
	1	4	
4			2

b)

	4	3	
1			2
	2	1	

c)

3			
			2

Can you circle the eight differences between these two images?

⏰ TIME ....

Can you draw seven of the loose dominoes onto the shaded tiles to complete this domino chain? One of the loose dominoes will not be used. Whenever two domino ends are next to one another, they must have the same number of dots.

Imagine rotating each of these shapes as shown by the arrow beneath it: 90° clockwise, 180°, and 90° anticlockwise as shown. Which of the options, 1 to 3, will result?

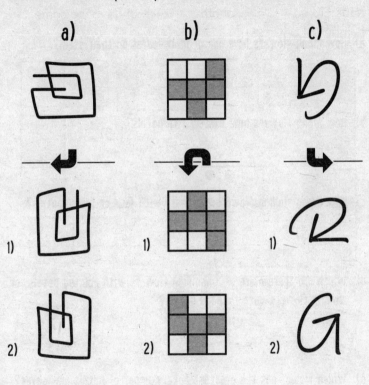

a)

b)

c)

1)

2)

3)

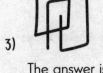The answer is:

The answer is:

The answer is:

....

....

....

Take a look at the flower creatures opposite, and answer the following questions as quickly as you can – then check more slowly to see if you were correct.

a) How many flowers have one or more leaves on their stem?

....

b) How many flowers have exactly five petals?

....

c) How many smiling flowers are there with four or fewer petals?

....

d) Which are there more of: unsmiling flowers with pointed petals, or smiling flowers with rounded petals?

....

e) Which flower has the greatest total number of petals and leaves?

....

f) What is the total number of petals on the top and bottom rows of flowers?

....

Take a look at the alien at the top of the page, then at each of the four possible silhouettes beneath. Can you circle the one silhouette which exactly matches the outline of the alien?

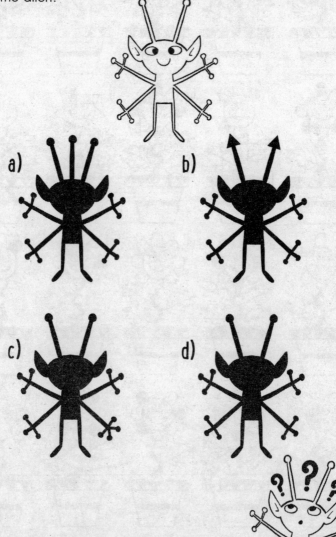

a)

b)

c)

d)

The shape at the top of the page has been hidden in one of the four images below, but which one? The answer must contain all of the black lines which make up the original image, but they may have been rotated – or had extra lines added.

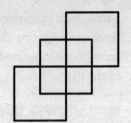

a)

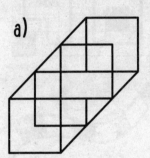

b)

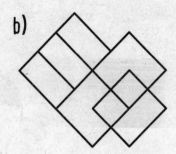

c)

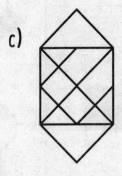

d)

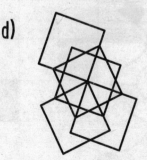

The answer is: ....

Draw lines to make a loop which visits every white square without using any diagonal lines, just like in the example solution below. The loop can't cross itself or use any square more than once.

Here's an example solved puzzle, so you can see how it works:

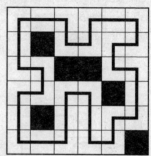

a)

Draw lines to join each pair of identical shapes, just like in the example solution below. Only one line can enter each square, and lines can't be drawn diagonally.

Here's an example to show what a complete puzzle looks like:

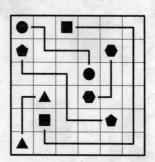

a)

Shade in each square according to the key below to reveal a hidden picture.

1 = light blue   2 = dark blue   3 = black

4 = yellow   5 = green   6 = red

7 = light grey   8 = orange   9 = brown

1	1	1	1	1	1	1	2	3	1	1	4	4	4	4
1	1	1	1	1	1	2	2	3	1	1	1	4	4	4
1	1	1	1	1	1	1	1	3	1	1	1	1	4	4
1	1	1	1	1	1	1	5	5	5	5	1	1	1	1
1	1	1	1	6	6	6	6	7	4	5	1	1	1	1
1	1	1	6	4	7	4	6	7	4	5	2	2	2	1
1	1	1	6	4	7	4	6	7	4	-5	7	4	2	1
1	1	1	6	4	7	4	6	7	4	5	7	4	2	1
1	1	1	6	4	7	4	6	7	4	5	7	4	2	1
1	1	1	6	6	6	6	6	5	5	5	2	2	2	1
8	8	1	1	1	3	1	1	3	1	1	3	1	1	8
1	9	9	9	9	9	9	9	9	9	9	9	9	9	9
1	1	9	9	8	9	9	8	9	9	8	9	9	9	9
2	2	9	9	9	9	9	9	9	9	9	9	9	9	2
2	2	2	9	9	9	9	9	9	9	9	9	9	2	2

How quickly can you find your way through this maze? Start at the arrow at the top.

Which of the three options, 1 to 3, is a perfect mirror reflection of the image on the left of each row?

a)

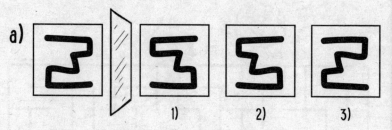

1)   2)   3)

The answer is: ....

b)

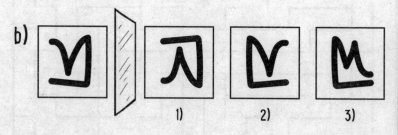

1)   2)   3)

The answer is: ....

c)

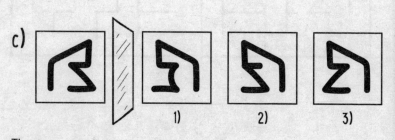

1)   2)   3)

The answer is: ....

Your friend has challenged you to pick up a selection of balloons whose numbers add up to various totals. Which balloons do you choose for each total? The first one is done for you as an example. Each balloon can only be used once per total.

Totals:

16 = ⑥ + ⑩   25 = ◯ + ◯ + ◯

19 = ◯ + ◯   28 = ◯ + ◯ + ◯

Join all of the dots with straight lines, starting at 7 (marked with a star) and then adding 7 at each step until you reach the final dot, which is hollow. What is revealed?

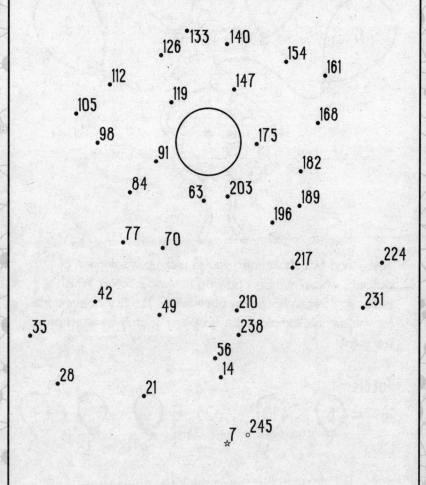

Can you find each of these twelve numbers in the grid?
They can be written in any direction, including diagonally,
and may read forwards or backwards.

182750	410847	514872	781053
238757	480474	601429	905028
34809	507309	604725	936552

9	7	9	9	7	5	3	5	5	8	9	8
2	4	0	2	5	5	2	5	4	5	5	2
8	1	5	4	7	2	2	7	4	0	7	2
6	8	0	5	8	1	7	9	7	8	2	7
4	2	2	5	3	3	9	3	4	5	4	9
7	7	8	5	2	4	0	1	2	8	7	3
8	5	5	7	8	9	5	7	0	3	9	6
8	0	4	0	7	9	4	1	5	2	2	5
2	4	4	8	0	0	4	0	4	6	8	5
9	7	7	8	6	2	1	1	0	2	9	2
4	8	4	1	4	8	0	6	3	7	1	5
8	3	3	7	7	6	8	2	9	9	0	0

Write 1, 2, 3, 4, 5 or 6 into each empty square so that no number repeats in any row, column or bold-lined 3x2 box.

Here's an example solved puzzle, so you can see how it works:

2	5	3	4	6	1
6	1	4	3	5	2
5	4	2	1	3	6
3	6	1	2	4	5
4	2	5	6	1	3
1	3	6	5	2	4

a)

5		2	3		4
1		4	5		2
	1			4	
	4			2	
6		3	4		1
4		1	2		6

b)

4		2	1		5
	1			4	
5	4			2	6
		6	4		
	5			6	
6		4	5		3

c)

1	6			5	2
5		2	6		1
	5			2	
	2			3	
3		5	2		4
2	4			1	3

How many squares, of various sizes (but not including rectangles), can you count in the following picture?

Don't forget the large one all around the outside!

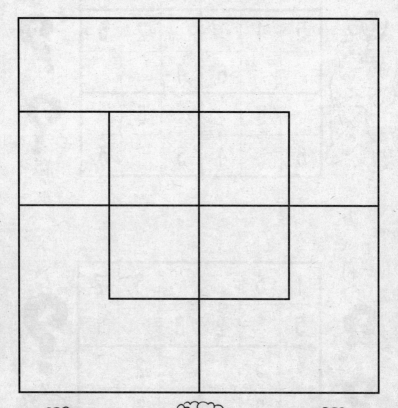

The answer is: ....

Which of the following shapes is the odd-one-out, and why?

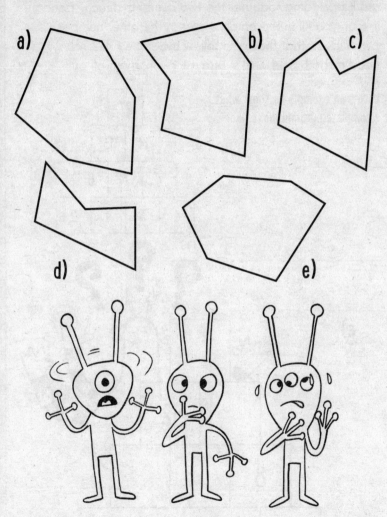

a)

b)

c)

d)

e)

The odd-one-out is _____ , because _____

....

In the number pyramid below, each number is equal to the result of adding together the two numbers directly beneath it. Can you fill in the empty boxes in the other number pyramids so that they also follow the same rule? You will need to both add and subtract to work them all out.

Here's an example to show what a complete pyramid looks like:

| 27 |
14	13
7	7	6
4	3	4	2

a)

| 12 |
| 8 |
| 2 | 6 |

b)

	32	
18		
	5	3

c)

16		
8		
	3	6

Start at the 'X' and then follow the arrows in the order given, moving one square in the direction shown for each arrow in turn. At which letter do you end up?

→ → ↓ → ↑ ↑ ← ← ← ← ↓ ↓ ← ↓ → → ↓ ←

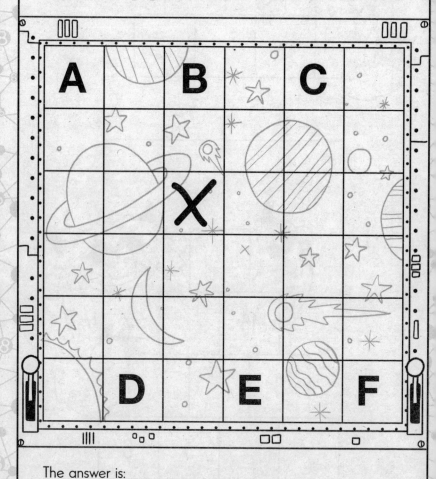

The answer is: ....

Starting on a circle which contains a 1, can you trace a route along the lines to 2, 3, 4, 5 and then 6 in that order, without visiting any number more than once?

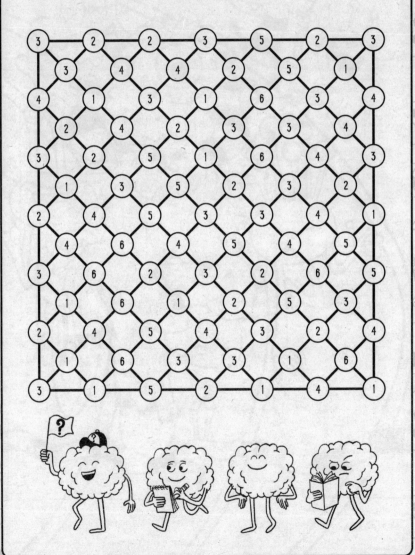

Can you circle the ten differences between these two images?

Draw over some of the dashed lines to join the circles into pairs. Every pair must contain one shaded circle and one white circle, just like in the example solution below. Every circle must be part of a pair of exactly two circles. The lines you draw must not cross over each other. They also can't cross over other circles.

Tip: Start with the circles that only have one other circle they could connect to.

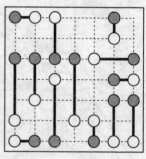

a)

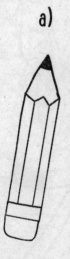

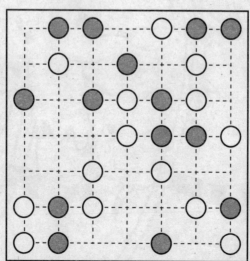

Write 1, 2, 3, 4, 5 or 6 into each empty square so that no number repeats in any row, column or bold-lined 3x2 box.

Here's an example solved puzzle, so you can see how it works:

2	5	3	4	6	1
6	1	4	3	5	2
5	4	2	1	3	6
3	6	1	2	4	5
4	2	5	6	1	3
1	3	6	5	2	4

a)

4 **3**

6			2		3
		5		4	6
1	6	4		2	
	5		6	1	4
4	3		5		
5		6			2

2 **1**

6 **5**

b)

6
3
5

3					1
	4	1	6	5	
	6			3	
	1			4	
	2	5	3	1	
1					2

2
1
4

c)

5
1
4

	3	6	4		
4					5
		3		1	
	1		6		
3					2
		2	5	3	

3
6
2

Can you draw either an 'X' or an 'O' into every
empty box of each puzzle so that no lines of 4 'X's
or 'O's in a row are formed in any direction,
including diagonally?

Here's an example solved puzzle,
so you can see how it works:

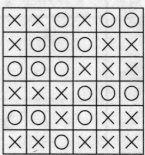

X	X	O	X	O	O
X	O	O	O	X	X
O	O	O	X	X	X
X	X	X	O	X	O
O	O	X	O	X	X
X	X	O	X	X	X

a)

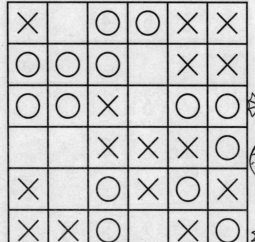

X		O	O	X	X
O	O	O		X	X
O	O	X		O	O
		X	X	X	O
X		O	X	O	X
X	X	O		O	

b)

×	×		○	○	○
×	×	○			
○		×		×	
	○	○	○	×	×
×	○	×		×	
×	×		×	○	×

c)

		○	○	○	
○				×	×
○	×	×	○	○	×
○	○	○	×	×	
					○
○	○	×	×		×

It's Nora's birthday today, and she has just turned 8.

a) How old will she be in six years' time?

.... years old

b) If Olly is half of Nora's age now, then how old was he this time last year?

.... years old

c) What is the current difference in age between Olly and Nora?

.... years

d) When Nora is 10, how old will Olly be?

.... years old

Can you work out which number should come next in each of the following mathematical sequences?

a) 17   14   11   8   5   ....

b) 320   160   80   40   20   ....

c) 19   28   37   46   55   ....

d) 5   15   24   32   39   ....

e) 243   81   27   9   3   ....

Take a look at the monster at the top of the page, then at each of the six possible silhouettes beneath. Can you circle the one silhouette which exactly matches the outline of the monster?

Shade in each square according to the key below to reveal a hidden picture.

1 = dark blue   2 = dark brown   3 = light purple

4 = red   5 = yellow   6 = orange

7 = black   8 = grey   9 = dark green

1	1	1	1	1	2	2	2	2	2	2	2	2	2	2	2	2	2	1	1
1	1	1	1	2	2	3	3	3	3	3	3	3	3	3	3	3	2	2	1
1	1	1	2	2	3	3	3	2	2	2	2	2	2	2	3	3	3	2	2
1	1	1	2	2	2	2	2	4	4	4	4	4	2	2	2	3	3	2	
1	1	1	2	2	2	4	4	4	4	4	4	4	4	4	2	2	3	2	
1	1	2	2	4	4	4	4	2	2	2	2	2	2	2	4	4	2	3	2
1	1	2	4	4	4	4	2	2	5	5	5	5	2	2	6	2	3	2	
1	1	2	4	4	4	4	2	6	2	2	2	2	2	6	2	4	2	3	2
7	1	2	4	4	4	7	2	6	2	5	5	5	2	5	2	6	2	3	2
7	7	7	4	7	7	7	2	6	2	5	2	5	2	6	2	4	2	3	2
1	7	7	7	7	7	4	2	6	2	5	2	2	2	5	2	6	2	3	2
1	7	8	7	8	7	4	2	6	2	5	5	5	5	2	2	4	2	3	2
1	7	7	7	7	7	4	2	6	2	2	2	2	2	2	6	6	2	3	2
1	1	7	7	7	7	4	2	2	6	6	6	6	6	6	6	2	3	2	
1	1	7	7	7	7	7	4	2	2	2	6	6	6	6	2	4	3	2	
1	1	7	7	7	8	7	7	4	3	2	2	2	2	2	4	3	4	2	
9	9	7	7	7	7	8	7	3	4	3	4	3	4	3	4	3	4	2	7
9	9	7	7	7	7	7	8	7	7	4	3	4	3	4	7	7	7	7	7
9	9	9	7	7	7	7	7	8	7	7	7	7	7	7	7	8	8	7	7
9	9	9	9	7	7	7	7	7	7	7	7	7	7	7	7	7	7	7	9

Can you find each of these twelve numbers in the grid? They can be written in any direction, including diagonally, and may read forwards or backwards.

292772	525770	663300	896232
424354	548966	723325	984410
44983	596693	773513	987338

0	0	4	9	6	8	2	3	5	9	2	6
6	7	3	5	9	6	8	9	8	4	4	4
8	7	8	9	2	3	9	0	2	9	2	9
7	5	9	2	6	5	1	8	7	7	4	2
4	2	7	8	9	4	3	4	4	7	7	4
5	5	3	6	4	2	9	5	3	5	6	2
3	8	3	8	3	2	3	8	9	3	7	7
4	1	9	8	3	9	0	1	7	7	9	6
2	2	0	0	3	3	6	6	5	3	3	8
4	8	9	6	2	3	2	5	5	3	3	4
8	8	4	3	3	9	6	6	9	5	7	8
4	3	3	3	5	2	3	3	2	7	3	7

Write 1, 2, 3, 4, 5 or 6 into each empty square so that no number repeats in any row, column or bold-lined 3×2 box. All even numbers (2, 4 and 6) must be written in the grey squares, while all odd numbers (1, 3 and 5) must be written in the white squares.

Here's an example solved puzzle, so you can see how it works:

6	3	2	1	5	4
1	5	4	2	6	3
3	1	5	6	4	2
4	2	6	3	1	5
2	4	1	5	3	6
5	6	3	4	2	1

a)

	3	2	4	5	
4		6			2
		5	1	3	
	1	4	6		
2			5		3
	4	3	2	6	

b)

	1			2	
2		4	6		5
	2			6	
	6			3	
6		2	1		3
	5			4	

c)

4			2		3
	3			5	
1		4	3		
		2	6		4
	4			3	
5		3			6

How many circles, of various sizes, can you count in the following picture?

The answer is: ....

BRAIN GAME 1

BRAIN GAME 2

13 = 6 + 7
17 = 8 + 9
21 = 6 + 7 + 8

BRAIN GAME 3

a)

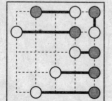

b)

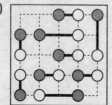

c)

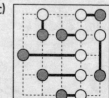

BRAIN GAME 4

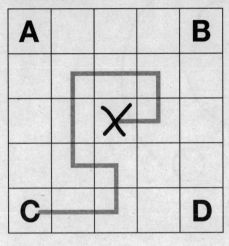

You end up at square 'C'

BRAIN GAME 5

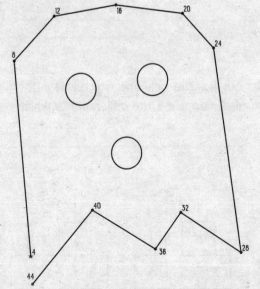

A ghost is revealed

BRAIN GAME 6

BRAIN GAME 7

11 is the odd number out. It is the only one which isn't in the 2-times table, which also means it is the only number which isn't even.

BRAIN GAME 8

a)
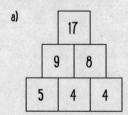

b)
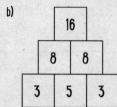

c)
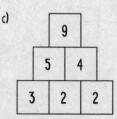

BRAIN GAME 9

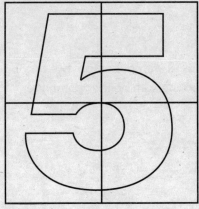

The answer is 5

BRAIN GAME 10

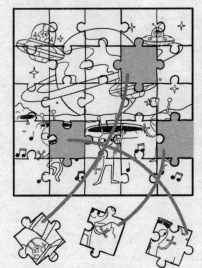
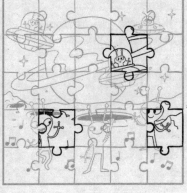

BRAIN GAME 11

a) 2: i and o

b) 3: b, j and k

c) 1: l

d) 5 more creatures. There are 10 with antennae, but only 5 with horns. There is also 1 creature with neither antennae nor horns.

e) 1: j

f) k: 14

BRAIN GAME 12

All of the shapes are regular polygons, meaning that they have all sides the same length and all angles the same, apart from e.

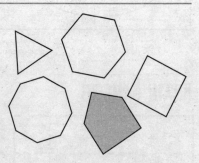

BRAIN GAME 13

BRAIN GAME 14

There are a total of 13 rectangles.

BRAIN GAME 15

a) Emma is Dexter's owner

b) Pickle has a red collar

c) Patrick's dog is called Pickle

Owner Name	Dog Name	Collar Colour
Sam	Rover	Green
Emma	Dexter	Blue
Patrick	Pickle	Red

BRAIN GAME 16

BRAIN GAME 17

a) 1
b) 3
c) 2

BRAIN GAME 18

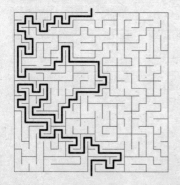

BRAIN GAME 19

BRAIN GAME 20

2 rectangles and 2 triangles

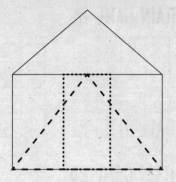

BRAIN GAME 21

a) 2
b) 3
c) 2

BRAIN GAME 22

a) 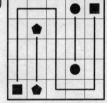 b) 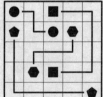 c)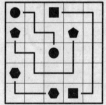

BRAIN GAME 23

a)

1	2	3	4
3	4	1	2
2	3	4	1
4	1	2	3

b)

2	3	1	4
4	1	3	2
1	4	2	3
3	2	4	1

c)

1	4	3	2
3	2	4	1
4	1	2	3
2	3	1	4

BRAIN GAME 24

a)
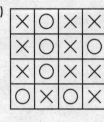

b)
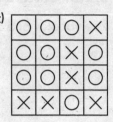

c)

BRAIN GAME 25

a)
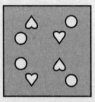

BRAIN GAME 26

a)

b)

c)

d)

The correct
silhouette is 'c'

BRAIN GAME 27

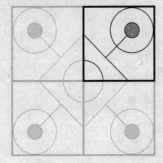

BRAIN GAME 28

BRAIN GAME 29

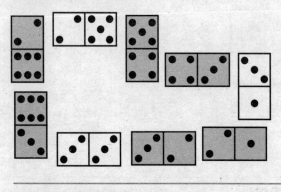

BRAIN GAME 30

a) 11 – add 2 at each step
b) 12 – subtract 2 at each step
c) 40 – subtract 10 at each step
d) 29 – add 5 at each step
e) 32 – multiply by 2 at each step

BRAIN GAME 31

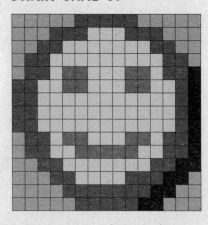

A smiley face is
revealed

BRAIN GAME 32

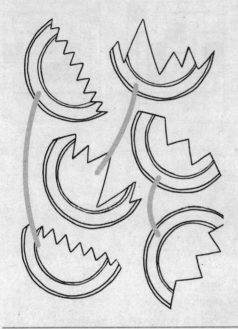

BRAIN GAME 33

b)

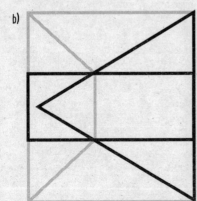

BRAIN GAME 34

a) 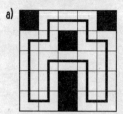 b) 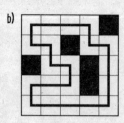 c)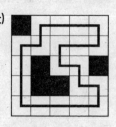

BRAIN GAME 35

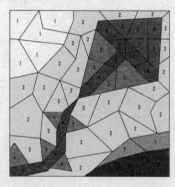

A flying kite is revealed

BRAIN GAME 36

BRAIN GAME 37

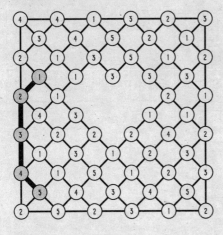

BRAIN GAME 38

a) 6 gold coins
b) 9 magic beans

BRAIN GAME 39

a) 3
b) 1
c) 3

BRAIN GAME 40

There are a total of 10 triangles (6 small and 4 large).

BRAIN GAME 41

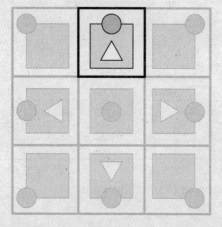

BRAIN GAME 42

10 is the odd number out. It is the only one which isn't in the 3-times table.

BRAIN GAME 43

BRAIN GAME 44

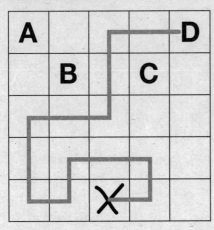

You end up at square 'D'

BRAIN GAME 45

11 = 5 + 6
13 = 6 + 7
18 = 5 + 6 + 7

BRAIN GAME 46

a)
O	O	X	O	X
O	X	X	X	O
X	O	O	O	X
O	X	X	X	O
O	X	X	X	O

b)
X	X	O	O	O
O	O	X	X	O
O	X	O	O	O
X	O	O	X	X
O	X	O	X	X

c)
O	X	O	O	O
O	X	O	O	X
X	O	X	O	X
X	O	X	O	X
O	O	X	X	O

BRAIN GAME 47

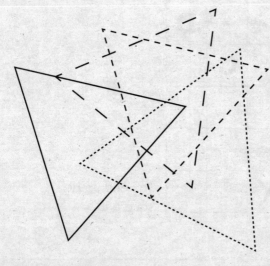

You would need to draw at least four triangles to recreate the image

BRAIN GAME 48

BRAIN GAME 49

BRAIN GAME 50

BRAIN GAME 51

a)

2	4	3	1
3	1	4	2
1	3	2	4
4	2	1	3

b)

1	4	2	3
2	3	4	1
4	1	3	2
3	2	1	4

c)

2	3	4	1
1	4	3	2
4	1	2	3
3	2	1	4

BRAIN GAME 52

All of the internal angles on the shapes bend inwards, apart from on shape 'e' where one angle bends outwards. You could also say that all the other internal angles are 'concave', which means they are less than 180 degrees, whereas in the highlighted shape one of the angles is 'convex', which means it is greater than 180 degrees.

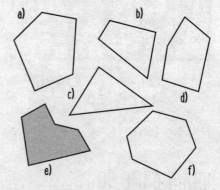

BRAIN GAME 53

c)

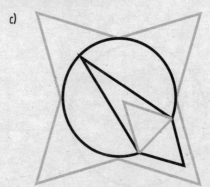

BRAIN GAME 54

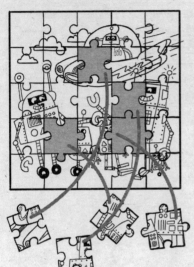

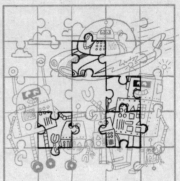

BRAIN GAME 55

BRAIN GAME 56

a) 1
b) 3
c) 2

BRAIN GAME 57

a)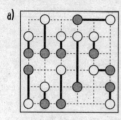

b)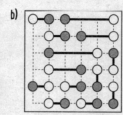

c)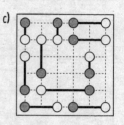

BRAIN GAME 58

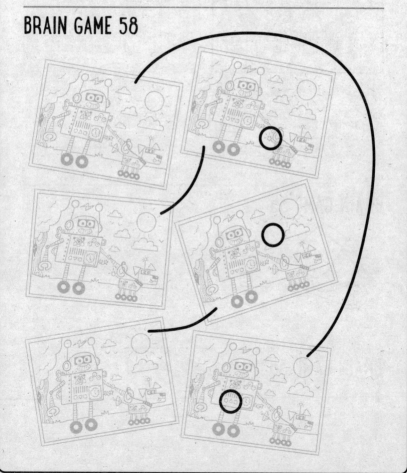

BRAIN GAME 59

BRAIN GAME 60

22 is the odd number out. It is the only one which is an even number (meaning it is in the 2-times table), while all the others are odd numbers.

BRAIN GAME 61

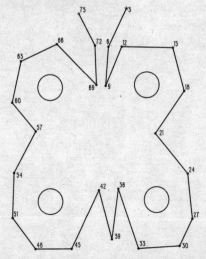

A butterfly is revealed

BRAIN GAME 62

a)
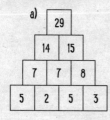

```
        29
     14     15
   7     7     8
 5     2     5     3
```

b)
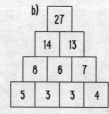

```
        27
     14     13
   8     6     7
 5     3     3     4
```

c)
```
        38
     20     18
   10    10     8
 5     5     5     3
```

BRAIN GAME 63

BRAIN GAME 64

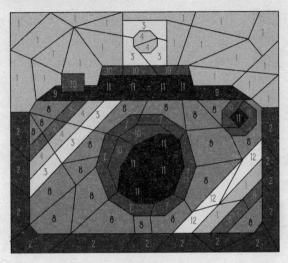

A camera is revealed

BRAIN GAME 65

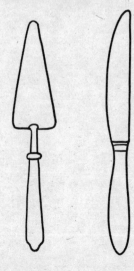

BRAIN GAME 66

c)

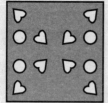

BRAIN GAME 67

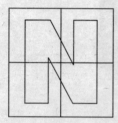

The letter is N

BRAIN GAME 68

BRAIN GAME 69

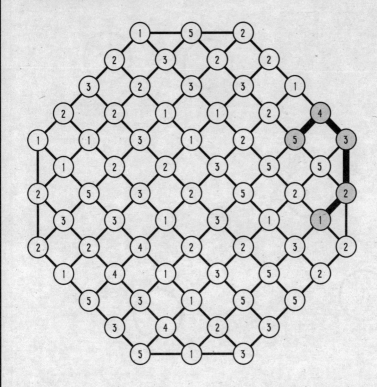

BRAIN GAME 70

a)

1	2	3	4
3	4	2	1
2	1	4	3
4	3	1	2

b)

2	4	3	1
1	3	4	2
3	1	2	4
4	2	1	3

c)

3	2	4	1
4	1	2	3
2	3	1	4
1	4	3	2

BRAIN GAME 71

BRAIN GAME 72

BRAIN GAME 73

a) 1
b) 3
c) 3

BRAIN GAME 74

a) 19: all except 'n'
b) 3: 'g', 'o' and 'p'
c) 1: only 'j' has four petals or fewer
d) There are more smiling flower creatures with rounded petals (13) than unsmiling flower creatures with pointed petals (1).
e) 'l'
f) 74

BRAIN GAME 75

a)

b)

c)

d)
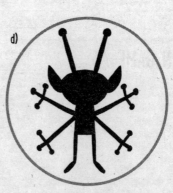

BRAIN GAME 76

d)
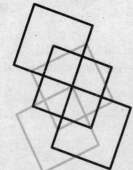

BRAIN GAME 77

a)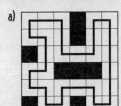

b)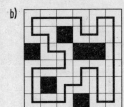

c)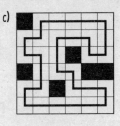

BRAIN GAME 78

a)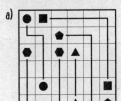

b)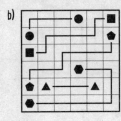

c)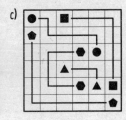

BRAIN GAME 79

A sailing boat is revealed

BRAIN GAME 80

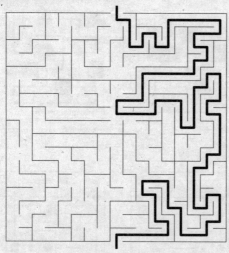

BRAIN GAME 81

a) 2
b) 2
c) 3

BRAIN GAME 82

19 = 9 + 10
25 = 6 + 9 + 10
28 = 6 + 10 + 12

BRAIN GAME 83

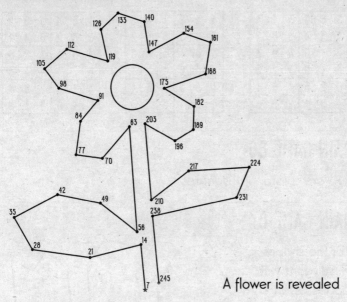

A flower is revealed

BRAIN GAME 84

9	7	9	9	7	5	3	5	5	8	9	8
2	4	0	2	5	5	2	5	4	5	5	2
8	1	5	4	7	2	2	7	4	0	7	2
6	8	0	5	8	1	7	9	7	8	2	7
4	2	2	5	3	3	9	3	4	5	4	9
7	7	8	5	2	4	0	1	2	8	7	3
8	5	5	7	8	9	5	7	0	3	9	6
8	0	4	0	7	9	4	1	5	2	2	5
2	4	4	8	0	0	4	0	4	6	8	5
9	7	7	8	6	2	1	1	0	2	9	2
4	8	4	1	4	8	0	6	3	7	1	5
8	3	3	7	7	6	8	2	9	9	0	0

BRAIN GAME 85

a)
5	6	2	3	1	4
1	3	4	5	6	2
2	1	5	6	4	3
3	4	6	1	2	5
6	2	3	4	5	1
4	5	1	2	3	6

b)
4	6	2	1	3	5
3	1	5	6	4	2
5	4	1	3	2	6
2	3	6	4	5	1
1	5	3	2	6	4
6	2	4	5	1	3

c)
1	6	4	3	5	2
5	3	2	6	4	1
4	5	3	1	2	6
6	2	1	4	3	5
3	1	5	2	6	4
2	4	6	5	1	3

BRAIN GAME 86

There are a total of 11 squares.

BRAIN GAME 87

All of the shapes are polygons with 6 edges, apart from 'd' which has only 5 edges.

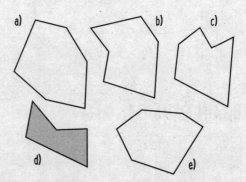

BRAIN GAME 88

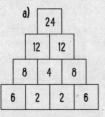

a)
```
        [ 24 ]
      [ 12 ][ 12 ]
    [ 8 ][ 4 ][ 8 ]
  [ 6 ][ 2 ][ 2 ][ 6 ]
```

b)
```
        [ 32 ]
      [ 18 ][ 14 ]
    [ 10 ][ 8 ][ 6 ]
  [ 5 ][ 5 ][ 3 ][ 3 ]
```

c)
```
        [ 33 ]
      [ 16 ][ 17 ]
    [ 8 ][ 8 ][ 9 ]
  [ 3 ][ 5 ][ 3 ][ 6 ]
```

BRAIN GAME 89

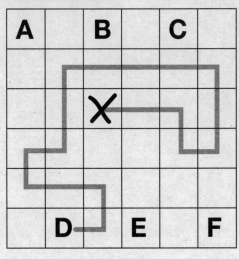

You end up at square 'D'

BRAIN GAME 90

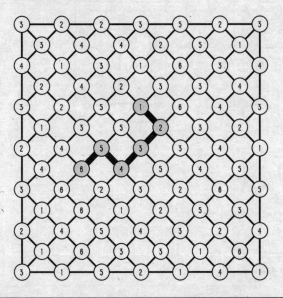

BRAIN GAME 91

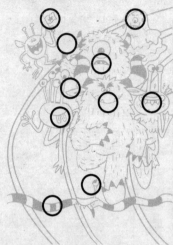

BRAIN GAME 92

a)

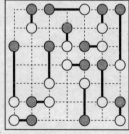

b)

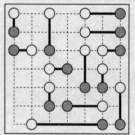

c)

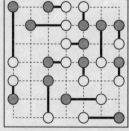

BRAIN GAME 93

a)

6	4	1	2	5	3
3	2	5	1	4	6
1	6	4	3	2	5
2	5	3	6	1	4
4	3	2	5	6	1
5	1	6	4	3	2

b)

3	5	6	4	2	1
2	4	1	6	5	3
4	6	2	1	3	5
5	1	3	2	4	6
6	2	5	3	1	4
1	3	4	5	6	2

c)

5	3	6	4	2	1
4	2	1	3	6	5
6	5	3	2	1	4
2	1	4	6	5	3
3	6	5	1	4	2
1	4	2	5	3	6

BRAIN GAME 94

a)

×	×	O	O	×	×
O	O	O	×	×	×
O	×	O	O	O	O
×	O	×	O	×	O
×	×	O	×	O	×
×	×	O	×	×	O

b)

×	×	×	O	O	O
×	×	O	O	O	×
O	O	×	×	×	O
×	O	O	O	×	×
×	O	×	×	×	O
×	×	O	×	O	×

c)

×	×	O	O	O	×
O	O	O	×	×	×
O	×	×	O	×	O
O	O	O	×	×	O
×	×	×	O	O	O
O	O	×	×	O	×

BRAIN GAME 95

a) 14 years old
b) 3 years old
c) 4 years
d) 6 years old

BRAIN GAME 96

a) 2 – subtract 3 at each step
b) 10 – divide by 2 at each step
c) 64 – add 9 at each step
d) 45 – add 10, then add 9, then add 8, then add 7, and finally add 6
e) 1 – divide by 3 at each step

BRAIN GAME 97

BRAIN GAME 98

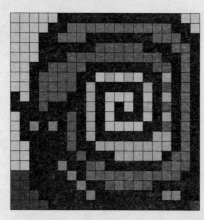

A snail is revealed

BRAIN GAME 99

0	0	4	9	6	8	2	3	5	9	2	6
6	7	3	5	9	6	8	9	8	4	4	4
8	7	8	9	2	3	9	0	2	9	2	9
7	5	9	2	6	5	1	8	7	7	4	2
4	2	7	8	9	4	3	4	4	7	7	4
5	5	3	6	4	2	9	5	3	5	6	2
3	8	3	8	3	2	3	8	9	3	7	7
4	1	9	8	3	9	0	1	7	7	9	6
2	2	0	0	3	3	6	6	5	3	3	8
4	8	9	6	2	3	2	5	5	3	3	4
8	8	4	3	3	9	6	6	9	5	7	8
4	3	3	3	5	2	3	3	2	7	3	7

BRAIN GAME 100

a)

1	3	2	4	5	6
4	5	6	3	1	2
6	2	5	1	3	4
3	1	4	6	2	5
2	6	1	5	4	3
5	4	3	2	6	1

b)

5	1	6	3	2	4
2	3	4	6	1	5
3	2	5	4	6	1
4	6	1	5	3	2
6	4	2	1	5	3
1	5	3	2	4	6

c)

4	1	5	2	6	3
2	3	6	4	5	1
1	6	4	3	2	5
3	5	2	6	1	4
6	4	1	5	3	2
5	2	3	1	4	6

BRAIN GAME 101

There are a total of 8 circles (4 in the middle, and 4 offset around the middle).

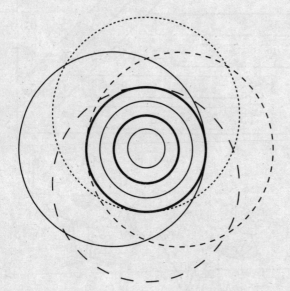

NOTES
AND
SCRIBBLES

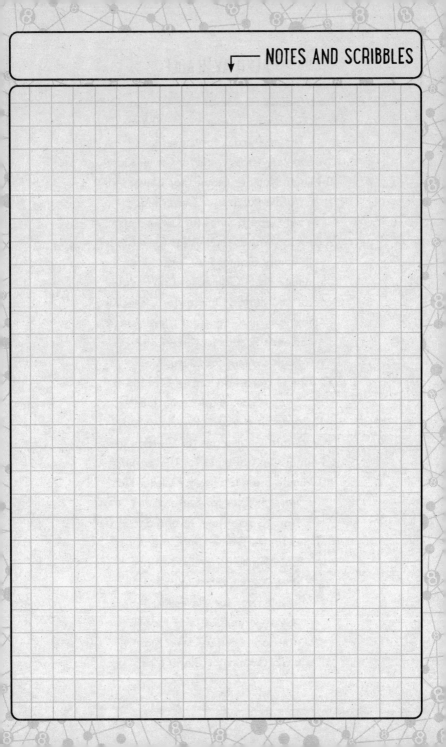

ALSO AVAILABLE: